A NOTE TO PARENTS ABOUT BEING RUDE

At the core of all rude behaviors is the perpetrator's belief that he or she is better than others. This misguided superiority complex often leads to feelings of entitlement. Rude people think they should be first. Rude people think they should have the best or the most. Rude people want to have their own way all of the time. Rude people need to be the center of attention.

No one likes to be around a rude person. This is the main reason parents do not want their children to be rude. They do not want their children to be disliked or ostracized by others. Being rude can also hurt people's feelings.

The purpose of this book is to help steer children away from rude behavior. By discussing this book with your child, you can help him or her behave in ways that garner positive rather than negative feelings from others.

If someone responds honestly to your child's rude behavior, you should not intervene. By allowing your child to suffer the consequences of his or her actions, you will allow him or her to learn what behavior is acceptable and what behavior is not acceptable.

A Children's Book About
BEING RUDE

Managing Editor: Ellen Klarberg
Copy Editor: Annette Gooch
Editorial Assistant: Lana Eberhard
Art Director: Jennifer Wiezel
Production Artist: Gail Miller
Illustration Designer: Bartholomew
Inking Artist: Rashida Tessler
Coloring Artist: Terry Magill
Lettering Artist: Linda Hanney
Typographer: Communication Graphics

A Children's Book About

BEING RUDE

By Joy Berry

GROLIER
B O O K S

GROLIER BOOKS IS A DIVISION OF GROLIER ENTERPRISES, INC.

This book is about Eric and his friends Lennie and Patty.

Reading about Eric and his friends can help you understand and deal with **being rude.**

You are being rude *when you treat other people as if they are not as important as you are.*

You are being rude *when you insist on being first.*

You are being rude *when you insist on having the best for yourself.*

You are being rude *when you insist on having the most for yourself.*

You are being rude *when you insist that everyone notice you and no one else.*

You are being rude *when you insist on having your own way all the time.*

When you are being rude, you are being selfish and unkind.

Other people might not want to be with you when you are being rude.

Try not to be rude. Do not insist on being first.

Wait patiently for your turn.

Try not to be rude. Do not insist on having the best for yourself.

Try not to be rude. Do not insist on having the most for yourself.

Try not to be rude. Do not insist that
everyone notice you and no one else.

Try not to be rude. Do not insist on having your own way all the time.

Avoid being rude by doing these things:

- Avoid saying anything that would hurt anyone.
- Avoid breaking or ruining anyone's things.
- Avoid talking while other people are talking.
- Avoid being noisy around people who need to have quiet.

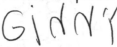

It is important to treat other people the way you want to be treated.

If you do not want people to be rude to you, you must not be rude to them.